The secret teachings of success and happiness combined with entrepreneurship, on how to create your passive income business and becoming a successful entrepreneur provides you all the necessary information about the author who started from being homeless to banker and a entrepreneur. It will train you first on your mindset about life and success, your mentality, self esteem, family, religion, fulfilling different perspective of your life which means on how to be educated, rich and smart on all perspective of life. And not just a product of a system getting good grades and having a huge depth or having a good job and neglecting your health or family by creating a individualistic family environment. Your eyes and brain will open to new information which will be your building block for your income, success, happiness and independence.

After that you will get information on different methods of earning money, and how to play it smart to increase your income and free time by putting more effort in the beginning. In the last chapters we will discuss the topics of saving while you have a job, investing in the stock market, starting a part time company and letting it grow to a self running business. And how to sell your business and retire trough Mergers and acquisitions.

Table of content

Introduction

About the author

The mindset of persistence and success

Education

Family and relationships as the fundamentals of success

What is investing

Saving and investing during your employment

Different types of entrepreneurs

Your company finance, marketing, web site and sales

Creating multiple sources of income with different companies and investments

Selling your company and retire or retire while having the company, about a exit strategy

Thank you word

Introduction

Dear reader, during 8 years of study at the university, investing in my free time and during my work at a bank I made the decision to write a practical handbook for young and older people about how to get most out of life. So that they will not make the same mistakes as I did and have the opportunity to be financially free as I am convinced that you are in a financial better position where I started as a homeless young man. A person want to be successful and wealthy for different reasons. Some people may invest or start a company to have more responsibility, to be their own boss, to gain financial freedom, to gain more wealth so that they could have a comfortable life, go on vacation and buy whatever they want in a short term. But It will take you time, effort and persistence to gain these privileges. It does not matter for which reason you do it, I sincerely believe that everybody should have a successful, comfortable and enjoyable life. When thinking about your work, savings or company. Think also about your whole life in different perspectives, you may have to get out of balance to achieve your goal. As long as it is short term it does not matter so that you can regain balance after weeks, moths or a few years. Some people are too much focused on work that they forget about their health, their family, their spiritual being and religion and lose themselves. These people may gain the world but as they did not do their best to bring consciousness and effort in all life perspectives they will still be losers. So read this book and make the best of it. Because of the crisis, unemployment and government cutting on retirement plans people are more reluctant to take their future in

GEORGE HORACE LORIMER- letters from a self made merchant to his son

"Before success comes in any man's life, he is sure to meet with much temporary defeat, and, perhaps, some failure. When defeat overtakes a man, the easiest and most logical thing to do is to quit. That is exactly what the majority of men do. More than five hundred of the most successful men this country has ever known told the author their greatest success came just one step beyond the point at which defeat had overtaken them." - Napoleon Hill

About the author

A long time ago a life of a young man started in the middle east. He was born in a Persian state, grown in a middle class family. The family were religious with strong norms and values, but it didn't matter how hard they tried the dictatorial government had put pressure on households by extreme political measure and by a weakened economy due to many reasons like mismanagement of the economical department and decisions. This family flee away because of economical disturbance in the 90's to a small European country. The young man grew and got older, as he got older he got interested in savings, interest and different interest rates in different countries. For example, if you put your money in a savings account in Germany, you would get a return on investment (ROI) on your savings account of 2%. But if you put your money in a savings account in lets say china, you would get 7%. But on the other hand if the currency of China devalues by 5,5 % that year, you will have a ROI of 1,5% which is lower than in Germany. So the young man started to read books about investing and different investment strategies. As he got to the point of going to the university, he made the decision to study international economics and business. During his study he invested in different companies with many gains and some losses. His losses were due his impatience, because these were actual good investments. He graduated from the university, started working in a bank for a short time. Got out of the bank and did more than 1200 applications.

He finally got a good job, saved and later on started his own firm in accounting and consulting and had multiple sources of income. But in all those years in his life, he made the choice in the type of life he wanted. Which was a good decent life bound by norms and ethical values. He improved life quality on different aspects like health trough sporting, family relationships, wealth by working, learning, saving, investing and entrepreneurship.

The mindset of persistence and success

In this chapter we are going to focus on persistence and success. There is a old saying about success which is:

"I'm convinced that about half of what separates the successful entrepreneurs from the non-successful ones is pure perseverance." - Steve Jobs

All people have their ups and downs in life, but the only thing that differs people is pure persistence. It is logical that some people are favored more than others, think about your background, family values, family status, money, the teachings of your parents and your environment. These will influence your chances on if you will become successful. But how come that there are many young men raised by good wealthy parents and they hanged on the streets and used drugs. And we also know about you men which had no family, money and status. But they found motivation and new ideas from the external environment and kept their persistence even in hard times. In the Koran there is written:

"Verily, man (disbeliever) was created impatient; irritable (discontented) when evil touches him; and niggardly when good touches him; except those who are devoted to salaah (prayers). Those who remain constant in their salaah (prayers)."

Many researchers and successful people like Napoleon Hill came up with the answer that the behavior of the successful and their persistence is the reason for their achievements. It is also well known in a branch of psychology on self esteem that you make decisions, based on your decisions you will have a certain outcome. And it is based on your outcome on how you feel and think about your self. For example in a ideological situation. You will go to school, do your best and study hard. Get a good degree and while you studies you work and have side activities to gain experience. And after a few years of work experience you climb up the management ladder. Besides this if you are religious with Jewish/Christian or Muslim norms and values you will behave in a good manner. Search for a spouse and get married in stead of just hanging around with people just for a short term enjoyment. The reason that this person is less successful than a person which you may know in your area is his way of doing things and the choices he made in life.

I will give a personal example: I was a young man, 22 years old doing a business and management study. I wanted to marry a girl which I knew from a long time ago. She is a far family member which I hadn't see her for years. I made the decision to do my best and get married with her before I achieve things in life like graduation and my first full time job. But the marriage didn't worked out, she had some personal problems which made it a wiser decision not to marry with her and I failed on my graduation thesis in the university. I was depressed, in such situation your vision (if you are a visionair) will break and you will have no clue what to do. Besides that I did some interviews so that I could start with my first real job in the banking sector before I graduate. Nobody hired me and many companies did not even respond. I remember when I was looking for a internship, I applied more than 120 times in for different internships, even abroad. But nobody hired me, but finally a recruiter found me somehow with the best internship which I could imagine in a investment department at a bank providing investment solutions for only wealthy people which is called private banking. So I started over again, corrected my thesis and rebuild my plans. This went so strong that I did additional accounting courses besides my job and a friend asked me to do his accounting for his company. Which was a solid base for my own future company and competencies. And concerning the wife, I revalued my needs and what I was looking for in a wife and corrected it with better and higher standards and start looking over again.

This is just an example of how things in life turn to be. A wise billionaire was very poor and went bankrupt, he was homeless. And somehow he managed to build everything and a company which made him a billionaire. He said: Things will be okay in the end, and if they still don't get okay, then it is yet not the end.

To make a conclusion, there is no such thing a failure. You will have a temporary defeat, and maybe multiple ones till you reach your goal. Your goal can be to work for your self, becoming a entrepreneur, creating a big self running company or becoming financially independent.

Education

When some of us had no education and some of us had a good education and a high university degree. I don't find anything educative in a diploma. Of course I went to the university and I learned different things. Thing which I could not learn If I did not went there. But that is because of the people I met. If I got the books and learned by my self I would get the same amount of information, maybe even better. That is exactly what I did, my education did not start and end in the university. I started to read educative books when I was 16 and never finished. While many people study medicine, to become a doctor or a accountant. The only thing which they can do I calculating or making medicine. They lack on other aspects of life. I have different skills which also includes IT skills. I can build a computer from different parts and install a software on it like mac or windows. These people are mostly programmed to do one thing, and they lack different skills, even in their personal lives. I will give you a example. My mother told me for finding a good wife, son that lady will be a good wife, she goes to the university. What type of rationalizing is that. At that time I still lacked some knowledge because it was before my gradation. But that same girl was not religious which means that she will lack some norms and values what holds the family ties together. She lived by her self on a young age, and worse than that she did not do that for the right purposes. And to make it even more dirty, she borrowed every month to live on her own while she was studying. I know that many people do that. But as it is written in the book: a guide to think clearly. And I acknowledge that point which is that if 50.000 people do something, that same thing is still bad. No matter how many people do that. So on other things about that girl is that she lacked cooking and household things. I saw her after she started to live by her self and she looked worse by the day. Well what type of mother will that be to my children and what profit will I have from having her as a wife! In stead such person can get educated on different life aspects, eating and living healthy. Adapting good religious values for her future, she will be the first one to make a profit out of it. And how to raise a child, many children now a days have psychological problems. One bus driver during the weekend told me that he is a teacher during the week. Some children had a hard time at school, and were not able to behave in a normal way. When they researched what the causes were, it became clear that those same children had mothers who worked. The children came home after school all alone and stayed till their mother came finally at 7 o clock at night.

So how I did my education. I saw that I lack money in my life and I need to become independent. So at a young age around 16 and 17 I learned about saving and even putting my savings in a other country because the interest rates were higher there. Interest is no go in Islam and there is a good reason for it, the rich get richer and the poor poorer, so I stopped later on. And I learned about investing in the stock market, how to analyze the stocks on fundamental and technical analysis and later on derivative products. Then during my study I saw that I was lacking a nice family home, My parents were divorced and I had no brothers and sisters. So the only way out and having a nice family was to start a successful marriage my self. So I started to read books about boundaries in the Christian and Muslim marriage. On how to be a good husband. Besides this I noticed that I lack stability in some psychological factors , and one of my friends was a child psychologist which I met at the student community. He advised me to read books on mindfulness, self esteem and later on I gained more knowledge about how to think positive. The reason that I am giving real life examples is to show you nothing comes for free, you have to become more conscious and greedy on knowledge to create a better life. During my study I worked as a sales person and I saw that the sales have to increase but I did not know how. So I started again and reeded different books about communication, nlp, marketing, sales and even hypnotherapy. Guess what, at that company I became famous for being a top sales person. And some years later I gained approximate 30% extra because of high bonuses, and no matter what I did at my job. My boss and colleagues liked me because I was the number 1 sales person in insurances in the whole area. After some years I wanted to start a company, I just graduated from the university with a business degree but I had no technical skills on anything. So I started doing a accounting course besides my job, and after that I realized that taxes are a high burden to employees and entrepreneurs. I reeded about multinational companies and how they avoid high taxes by international tax treaties. So I followed a one and half year tax course. During the day I worked in the evenings and weekends I went to the gym and learned about taxes. I rebuild my self by that time and wanted to learn about different ways to invest, so I found a free workshop on real estate investing and learned some new things and tactics.

So educate your self, on you personal circumstances and your basic life which comes naturally. And educate your self about marketing, advertising sales. How different entrepreneurs started. How you can be financially free. It sounds tiring because you have to do all this research and reading. But it comes with the time, time is going no where, you get older by the day and you might spend it in a wise manner. Weather it is entertainment, relaxation, education or work. Spend your time effective, efficient and wisely. You will have a long life so you can start now and over a few yours you will look back on how much knowledge you have gained by that time when every body else did nothing. I also want to let you know that you should not become too greedy and materialistic, because then you will lose your self. And forget your life purpose, money and work are just tools to have a better fulfilling life son that you may spend more on charity, spend time with your family and enjoy life in a good way.

As a conclusion, life has different aspects. You can look at a thing in 2 ways or you can look in 3d and see what the other aspects are. So you may want to bring more consciousness on your friends and relationships, your marriage, your finances, healthy eating habits and going to the gym. Which somebody told me all those things, it would spear me a lot of effort finding things out by my self.

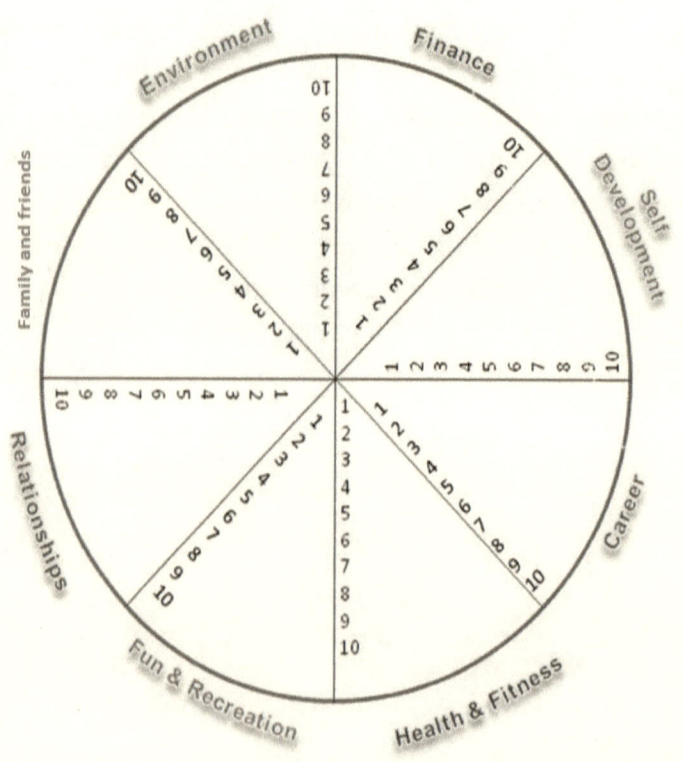

Family and relationships as the fundamentals of success
Family and human interactions as you fiend in friendship
and relationships is a very important fundamental for
success and a happy life. Why is this? Let say in a utopia
that you have a huge sum of money on your bank
account, but you lack a family, friends, a spouse and
colleagues. You will purchase new things, go on nice all
inclusive trips. But after a while you will realize that these
materialistic goods will not give you the satisfaction you
need. But as I remember, I come from a middle class
family. Me and my father and mother played games
together when I was a child. We went on trips, my father
learned me haunting. And these are the small things
which bring you joy. Besides this, when starting a
company you will go trough a lot of ups and downs. You
are not at the same safe place as when you work in a team
in a company. Its a lonely and hard road. But when you
have your wife, family and friends they will support you
when you are down. And when everything is going good,
and you have money in abundance. You can share this
blessing with your spouse, family and friends. Just a
practical example, I am good at financial things, in my
free time I learned the tricks for your tax returns as a
professional tax advisor. And I did a extra study after my
university degree to become a professional tax advisor.
When I finished my own tax return papers, I helped a
friend which never got money back from the tax agency in
the past. And after doing his paper work and finding the
gaps, like study deduction on your tax payment. He got a
nice tax refund, of course he was happy with this. He
could use it as a savings or use it for him self and his wife.

These human relationships are very expensive and you should cherish them. Unfortunate we live in a individualistic society specially because its the 21 century in the western world. Everybody seeks his/her own profit and forgets that we live in a group society and as it is with animals it is with us. They are weak by them selves, but in a group they are strong.

The second part is the networking part, to be honest I don't believe in this part but I will still explain this topic. When you go to networking events or you know people from different field areas, this can be a huge plus when you have your own company. It will save you time and money when asking for help. But I was active in the politics, I did a internship at a bank and I know people from different backgrounds. But I never asked those people for any help in my life, and neither could they be a help for me. Because at a networking event, the name says everything about it. Everybody comes for his/her own profit to do some networking. They are not social workers in old clothes trying to explain and help you. But rather ego centric individualistic human beings spending time in these network areas to fulfill their gap which they have created in their personal lives.

What is investing

We first have to start understanding what investing means and different ways to invest. Investing means using your (accumulated) wealth in different products/companies in the hope that those products gain in price. Well for which reason does a product gain in price? When a there is a high demand in a certain product and less offers the price will be higher that a product which has a low demand with a lot of producers/sellers and offers. We could use an example, strawberries usually grow in the summer. Which means that many tailors will produce strawberries and you will have a high quantity of offers at the market. Lets say that a small box of strawberries will cost 1 Euro equivalent to 1,4 dollars at the currency rate in 2014. In the winter the strawberries are usually sold out, a proportion will rot and the rest which was plucked in the beginning of the winter will be less in terms of quantity. When you go to the same market in the winter you will see that there are less sales people selling those strawberries. But the usual household would like to purchase the same amount of strawberries. Which will mean that due to weather conditions those strawberries will be harder to produce. The price of a small box of strawberries will be 1,95 Euro or higher. And the salesman will actually sell those products for that price. When this economic model counts for a pack of goods or fruit it also counts for the stock market and real estate price. Even when the company doesn't have the good business model, if there is a high speculation and need for those stocks because people believe in that company, it will still gain value.

In the past our grandparents would save money and keep this in old socks, which is partially true if I look at my own grandmother. But nowadays you could save that money or even borrow it and put it in a place where people need it. What does that mean? Some companies want to expand, or purchase new machines. In order to make to investments they need capita. The capital could be financed by different ways, the company could borrow money from the bank and pay a certain amount of interest or they could issue stocks. Where small and big investors like pension funds will purchase their stocks and gain a piece in that company. The company then has the ability to purchase different machineries to produce more and expand which could lead to higher returns. And that return will theoretically be recalculated in a higher stock price. When you sell that higher stock price in the future, it will have a higher value than your original investment.

Below I will explain different tools wealthy people use to accumulate more wealth.

Stocks

Stocks are a piece of a company, lets say the company has 1000 dollars worth of machines, a brand that is not known by many and is worth 500 dollars. On the bank account of the company there is 500 dollars and they have a small loan worth 300 dollars which was needed for purchasing those machines. The total amount which the company is worth is 1000+500+500-300= 1700 dollars. Lets say that the company has 1 owner which did not spend any penny on the company but many shareholders. The virtual company will have 17 share holders, each shareholder invested 100 dollars in the company in the hope to gain more wealth. When the company wants to expand they will issue new stocks, lets say that they need another 300 dollars for a machine. They will therefore issue 3 other stocks on the stock market which I will explain later on. You as a investor will contact your bank and buy 3 stocks each worth 100 dollars. If the company gains a higher profit in the future and many other people want to purchase the same stocks, they will call their bank, or make a electronic transaction trough internet banking and purchase your stocks if you want to cash in. The computers at the stock market will calculate that the share price will be worth 150 dollars each for the good profits of the company and the high demand. You will therefore make 3x50 dollar (profit)= 150 dollar profit on a investment of 300 dollar which is 50%. The stocks, and prices are listed on the stock market. Each country has a stock market and it is possible to invest in a stock market in a different country, you usually need a currency bank account or a separate abroad stock account. In the US there are different stock exchanges, the biggest is NYSE, which is called New York stock exchange. And the smaller companies have a rating on another exchange list called the S&P. In the Netherlands the biggest companies are listed on the AEX, all the stock prices which are listed on that are calculated. The AEX has also a rating made trough all those stock prices, It is currently rated on 413 Euro. But that still means that if you want to buy a share in Shell, it will cost you 23 dollars per piece and not 413. In the past you got a piece of paper written on it how much shares you have in that company. But now the purchase and sales of those stocks are now done virtually by computer calculations, and you will see the amount of shares and price per share digitally on your internet bank account. Usually you have to pay the bank a small fee of lets say 3 dollars if you want to buy those stocks. You have to pay that fee for their service, because as a small investor you are not able to purchase stocks directly on the stock exchange, but you will do this trough your bank or broker. Your broker will spend time to buy those shares and settle it on your bank account. You can buy stocks even when you have 100 dollars, but it will be wise to start with a minimum amount of 1000 dollars. The reason for that is that have to pay the bank a fee of 3 Euro for their service which means that it counts for 3 percent profits if you buy for 100 Euros.

Bonds

Bonds are a piece of paper stating that the company owes you. When a company or government wants to borrow money they can issue bonds, usually worth 1000 dollars each and pay interest on that. The interest is made trough the credit rating. If the company has a low liquidity, low savings, bad product and is not well known the rating agencies give a low rating like C, which means that you will get a higher interest, lets say 8%. But this also means that you are willing to take higher risks. Those bonds are also listed on the bond exchange. On the issuing date each bond price is 1000 dollars worth, with a interest rate of lets say 5%. But is the demand will be low in the future due to higher risks which will be said on the news, the bond price could decline and the interest rate therefore has to increase to attract investors. Some investors purchase those bonds and keep them till maturity date, which is the end date of those bonds, that could be 1 year or 10 years. But some purchase those bonds when it is economically going bad with the company, the bond price is then low with a high interest rate. But they keep that bond for a short while and sell it when the company gives good news about higher profits they earned and for example low interest rates of the savings account. Then it is more attracting to invest in that bond price, and while many people want to buy those bonds instead of keeping their money on a low savings account. The short term investor will sell his bonds for a higher price.

Saving and investing during your employment

When you want to start your company you want to reduce the risk of default. You want to be successful, have a good life and provide a good product or service to your customer and the society as a whole. So before starting your company it is important to gain knowledge about the product/service, market and the daily tasks. Of course you can not oversee everything, you should not even bother. But when you have some experience this will be a huge advantage for you and your company. The first practical thing is to save money when you work somewhere. This will give you the opportunity to start planning, gathering information, finance and the basics to start your company while you have your steady paycheck. Save as much as you can, because starting a company will create different costs and you will have to pay for it and reduce the amount you need to borrow. The costs can be the costs of the chamber of commerce, website, utilities, overhead, office, machines, computer, printer, an accountant and marketing etcetera. This will also give you the opportunity to start a part time company while you are working somewhere. Of course you will not have much time and you will have to sacrifice a lot to focus on your company in your free time but it will be a advantage.

Different types of entrepreneurs
*Self employed
*Big businesses
*Investor

As Robert Kiosaki says it, there are different type of entrepreneurs.
The first type of entrepreneur is the self employed entrepreneur, it could be a free lancer or a solo man working. As a freelancer you could get hired by a company but without the benefits of normal employees. Some self made entrepreneurs are consultants with a special knowledge in a certain field or they provide a service or product. When you are self employed, there is a huge pressure on you because you have to do everything on your own. The success of your company depends on your personal, technical and communication skills. You have to know about everything a little. Sometimes you have to outsource some tasks to a third party like a accountant or tax advisor because this requires a certain type of knowledge and skills. These types of entrepreneurs or more dependent on their family and friend.

There are the middle and big businesses. Well no business starts big, you will have to purchase a existing company/formula or you will have to start a company with different people. This has its pro's and con's. You are more dependent and you will not be able to make full decisions but the positive added value about this is that you and your partner in business will fulfill each others gaps. Currently I am setting up a business with friend . I am a hard working analytical person with financial and sales skills. But that friend has creative and marketing skills. Those two combined will create a good force to set up a business. He will come with different solutions and I will analyze and fill up the technical gaps. When you have 10 accountants starting a business there is a waste of time. They don't add value towards each other with different skills and knowledge. When you have such a company it is more likely that your company grows as you take strategic decisions and outsource different tasks. These entrepreneurs can do little or no work and enjoy their spare time if they hire the right people. But before expanding it is important that your revenue or easy said "your income" has to be higher than your expenses because you have to hire different people to do the task for you.

And at last we have the investor. These investors saved or acquired huge amount of capital and they are able to spend or invest this. There are different ways they invest their money. Recently I went to a workshop about real estate investing. They buy houses and rent them to generate cash flow, which is a steady monthly income. This investment will also increase most likely in value because it is a real estate investment if you purchase it at the right moment at the right place and condition. There are also investors who buy government bonds and stocks. If you want to get the technical skills to make money with these investment you can look up my other books on Amazon, Lulu or Kobo. And at least we have the investors which are called angel investors, they invest in companies and startups. These startups need cash to start or to grow. The angel investors provide them with cash for a steady annual return or a share in the company.

Your company finance, marketing, web site and sales
Now we are going to elaborate about the practical matters
concerning you business. This is one of the most
important parts because your strategy and knowledge on
these topics can lead you to become a winner or lose in
the game of entrepreneurship. But remember that one of
the things that separates the successful and the non
successful is pure persistence. You do not need to be a
professional marketeer, accountant, web designer and
sales person at the same time. Mostly entrepreneurs hire
people do do those jobs for them. But when you lack
funds, then you have to make the start on your own. I did
a business degree so for me most of those topics were
teached in class, but my real lesson began when I
graduated. Then I started to really take responsibility and
expand my knowledge on these parts to reduce my cost
and even gain something out of it.
Finance

We discussed earlier that it would be wise if you saved and invested your money, so that you can have a small fund to start with. Mostly this will be not enough. Just think about the example for a trade startup. When you trade goods you will have to purchase stock (e.g. purchase the goods which you want to sell), you will have to pay for stalling the goods and the transport. Not even included the cost of marketing, accountants and lawyers which you do business with. There are different possibilities to borrow money. Once a wise man said, entrepreneurs use OPM (others peoples money) to add value to the society. But there is a catch, Interest which is paid on the money borrowed, is a dirty type of business. From ancient times wealthy people get wealthier by lending their money to borrowers with a high interest rate. While a average salary increase (not even taking in to account the risk of losing a job or go bankrupt) is 2%. But the average interest rate from the bank is 8%, and even the credit card interest rate is around 13%. These percentage are mostly even compounded interest rates, which means that you do not pay 13% on a yearly basis. But rather pay 13:12 months= 1,08333% each month. But because you pay interest over interest after 12 months it is not 13% but 13,08%. Below there are different ways to find investments for your company.

*Savings
*Bank credit/loan
*Family
*Crowd funding platform
*Angel investor

There are different web sites where you can find crowd funding platforms. These platforms are where people choose startups and invest in a certain startup. But the amount per investor is small, all those small amounts sum up to huge amounts of savings which is invested in to your company. As a return you will give them your product, percentage of the company, interest rate or a part of your profits.

Below you will find many web sites for only The Netherlands.

http://www.douwenkoren.nl/crowdfunding-in-nederland/#oa

http://www.crowdfunding.nl/crowdfunding-platforms/

https://www.ikgastarten.nl/financi%C3%ABn/crowdfunding/5-nieuwe-nederlandse-crowdfunding-platforms

http://www.sprout.nl/artikel/hier-haal-je-als-ondernemer-crowdfunding

http://www.geldenondernemen.nl/crowdfunding.html

An angel investor/venture capitalist/informal investor is a wealthy person mostly a retired entrepreneur who is looking for alternative way of growing his savings. The angel investor either invests in you because he is looking for a steady annual return, a gain in value or a part of your great company.

http://www.bannederland.nl/

http://www.venturemedia.nl/Angel-investor

http://www.mindhunter.nl/

http://www.investormatch.nl/investeerders-aangeboden

https://www.angelinvestmentnetwork.nl/

When starting you business it would be wise to write a business plan. A business plan is a paperwork where you sum up what your product or service is, who your target group is, how your finances, marketing and sales will be. You can even write a short 20 pages business plan which you can show to the investors and look up in your self for refreshment. In the financial part and even when you are running your business. You will have to show your cash flow to the local tax agency to know what your income, assets and liabilities are.

In the balance sheet you will state your assets and liabilities, which means the products that you intended to buy or purchased and the way you financed them.

The left part is your assets and the right part is the way you financed them. These two parts should have the same amount.

Balance sheet

Assets		Liabilities	
Computer	500,-	Loan	150,-
paper	10,-	Savings	200,-
printer	50,-	Family	300,-
desk	100,-	crowd.f.	1050,-
machinery	240,-		
shoes for sale	800,-		
Total	1700,-		1700,-

You will also have to report a annual income/loss statement to the local tax authorities. Or your accountant will do that because there are many regulations which a entrepreneur does not know and should not even bother. In the Netherlands you will have to report every quarter a VAT report and in the beginning of the next year you will have to report your income tax deducted by your costs.

Income statement 2015

Income		Costs	
Advise	23000,-	Marketing	200,-
Freelancer	12000,-	products	1700,-
		Web site	50,-
Total	35000,-		1950,-

The Net income will be 35000 – 1950= 33050,- Net income. Your accountant will calculate your tax deduction offer which is +/- 3000,- for a self employed and 7000,- for a starter for the first tree years. Which is 33050,- - 10000,- = 23050,- Taxable income. You will pay approximate 30% of 23050,- for your yearly tax payment.

Marketing

What is marketing? Marketing is advertising techniques which can lead to a increase of customer awareness and higher sales. Marketing is very important for a company, many companies don't hold savings but put their savings in advertising and marketing costs. The reason for this is because when you reach a new customer, he or she will not only be a customer but may do repeated purchases over time which will lead to a steady sale on the long term. I know a Chinese mobile brand which my colleague advised me on. I saw that mobile in the hands of my colleague, customers and even in the gym I saw people holding that mobile. When I asked them about it they explained me with enthusiasm about the good specifications and that they sell it for a very good price 300 Euros. This mobile is only sold by mouth to mouth words and it is not being directly advertised. Here you see how a company can build a strong brand value. There are different advertising methods. In this part we will clarify different types of advertising. Some types of advertising are traditional offline like the newspaper and some are online. The first important thing is who is your target group. This is very important because it will give you the opportunity to spend your money on advertising reaching more potential customers. An example if you target young sportive males for Nike t-shirts you rather advertise at tennis and football clubs in stead of advertising to a group of hard working social workers who are more busy with charity than sports.

*your target group

Then there are different types of advertising methods.
Online:
Facebook
Twitter
Blog
Web site
Google (ad words)

Offline:
Bus stations
Newspaper
Magazines
Door to door brochures
Sales people
Networking days

Social media i.e. online advertising is very important.
Special for the new millenia or the Y generation. The
young people spend a lot of time reading articles and
searching information on the internet. The online sales are
even increasing, people tend to shop more online year by
year in stead of going to a store unfortunate. It reduces
social contact but thats for a other time of philosophical
discussions.

Social media is getting more and more important in our daily lives. When I look at my self, when I come from work the time I spend on the internet. Is the time on looking up information trough different channels. You can make a facebook page of your company and every week write a small article to keep fans up to date. The same counts for twitter and a blog. These 3 combined will lead customers from one to another web site of yours. You will first add friends to your facebook page and after a while you can follow different target groups on twitter, they will more likely follow you 2. This will increase the brand awareness your creating. These type of advertising are free or very cheap. While you can also do local advertising at bus stops, news papers and magazines. You just need to contact them and write a nice article with a picture of your company. The costs will vary between 20,- and 300,- Euros.

A very common used word in marketing is the 4p's. These are:
Product : Which product or service are you going to sell
Price : For which price
Place : Where is the place where you want to sell your product/service
Promotion : Trough which channels are you going to do your advertising

I would like to end this part with a extra type of information which is taboo in explanation. In marketing many big companies use dirty tricks in the hope to gain a higher sale. For example: NLP which stands for neuro linguitic programming. Scientific tools for example in a advertising a person takes the bottle with the right hand because most people are right handed. Ads and logos upside down, I saw one of the advertisements of Nike with a upside down text of a Islamic text. One of the best universities in The Netherlands (Erasmus) uses Horus and the eye of Ra on their internal Blackboard web site where students can find information. Horus and Ra are old Egyptian deities, so why are these placed as a picture on the web site for students? These could look to some people to conspiracies, whatever they are they are made and advertised weather you want it or not. Be aware of it and distance your self from it. The honor of a man is when he provides a product or service which will be a added value to a society. Then he will prosper and the society as a whole will consume that product because of its value, so not by using mystical theosophical magic advertisement. Be open and clear about your product or service.

Web site

You can either outsource the web site to a real web site developer. Or if you are tight on your budget you can make a easy web site your self. You just need to go to www.wordpress.com . You can make a free web site. The design is already made and you can choose which one you want. After that you can Google: buy a host name. This is a name by which you want to be found with. For example: www.hello.com is a host name. You will link your wordpress web site to your host name. And your host name will consist of your company name or product. A host name will cost you around 10,- Euros per year. So this is the cheapest way to make a web site.

Creating multiple sources of income with different companies and investments

After Starting your company and running it you could think about the first thing which I explained. So not being self employed but let other people run your business and do the tasks which you need to do. Then you will have more time to spend more time to start a new company or a new source of income. This is important because I saw many companies go bankrupt when focusing on one product or group. When the market is saturated or there is a crisis in that branch of business you will lose your income.

There are different ways to create multiple sources of income, for example purchase a company which is called mergers and acquisitions. It is however smart to do good research about that company and have some experience or knowledge in that field.

Giving other the chance to run your company, there are many students who are more than willing to do tasks in your company for a low salary. They have fresh knowledge and it is wise to ask them for input to increase the productivity in your business.

There are ways to purchase and sell products, for example many years ago I purchased a car for 500 Euros and after using it for a few moths I sold it for 800 Euros. This is just a small example that there are different opportunities to purchase goods at a lower price and sell them at a higher price.

Real estate was and still is a good business. There are real estate investors which purchase a house and resell that for a higher price or rent it. In the past I went to a workshop about real estate investing and one of those people was a real estate goroe as I call him like that. He has multiple houses and buildings and rented those. The only negative past is that if you do not own the capital to do that you will have to borrow. He borrowed at a interest rate of 1,2 percent per month which will be slightly above 14% per year. That is a abnormal high interest rate. I guess that is one of the reasons why in religion they say that interest is not accepted. It kills the opportunity to grow and save.

Selling your company and retire or retire while having the company
About a exit strategy

After years of finding the right product or service. And providing that, your company most likely will grow. Weather you are self employed or created a business where people work for you, you can choose to sell your company. Remember that you have to make a strategy for having something to do after that. It could be a world trip, retiring, free work or a new project and a new company.

There are different workshops and local networking days for selling or purchasing a company. In the Netherlands there is something called Nationale Overnamedag. Many companies come there to show their business which they want to sell. There are also good prospects who are interested in purchasing a company.

Brooks is also a Dutch web site where more that 10.000 professionals, sellers and buyers come and meet online. Besides that there are different companies who are specialized in M&A which stands for Mergers and Acquisitions, they differ from small to big companies with a specialized know how about the legal and financial aspect of selling and purchasing a company. You can find your local advisor by one of my best friends called www.google.com. Here are different companies who advice you in the Netherlands like: Marktlink, RTL ventures, Deloitte, Ernst and Young, Grand Thornton, KPMG, Mazars, Wingman business valuation.

In the past it was easy to set a price on a company, entrepreneurs would say 5 or 7 times the yearly earnings. But now it is harder to calculate the price of a company. There are different formulas for setting a price, some use 'discounted cash flow' as a example. But if they are 9000% in dept and have a good sales figure, that is still not a good option. So it is important to take the following in to consideration:

What are their:
-Assets
-Liabilities e.g. depth
-Know how, knowledge of the employees
-Steady income? Like a accountancy firm
-Growth possibilities and future growth potential
-Strategy
-Customers
-Sales
-Net profit before and after tax
-Company structure in case of bankruptcy

Thank you word

Remember that starting and building a company is like a journey. You should not see it as a task. Enjoy that journey, because you will learn and meet new people during the way. When you use your competencies and feel in your element, that is the moment when you are the most productive and successful. Because you do what you like and that you are good at in a playful way.

I hope this book provided you with all the necessary basic information about how to start, grow and sell your business. You could always read more in depth about different things which I mentioned in this book. A wise man once said that a person with low self esteem tries and falls and never tries again. A person with a high self esteem is so persistent that he will try till he finally does not get defeated. And I did not mention winning, but not being defeated! I wish you good luck, enjoyment and wealth in the future.

www.ingramcontent.com/pod-product-compliance
Lightning Source LLC
Chambersburg PA
CBHW021446170526
45164CB00001B/417